SOLOMON
A KING IS CROWNED

King David was very old and frail. He had ruled over Israel for forty years. Now it was time for him to choose a new king.

One day, Adonijah, who was a son of David, decided to make himself king. This made Bathsheba, one of David's wives very worried. 'Didn't you say that our son, Solomon, would be the next king?' she said to David. 'Now Adonijah has made himself king and Solomon and I will be treated very badly by him.'

King David listened thoughtfully. 'I made you a promise and I will keep it,' he said. He called Zadok the priest and Nathan the prophet to him and said, 'Take my son, Solomon, to the place called Gihon. He is to travel on my mule. When you get there, take a horn of oil and anoint him king.'

So the two men did as David had commanded and Solomon was made king. Trumpets sounded and the people played flutes to celebrate. 'Long live King Solomon!' they shouted.

When David heard that his son was king he was very pleased. But Adonijah was frightened. Perhaps Solomon - the real king - would kill him?

Solomon, however, was kind and wise. 'If he is a worthy man he will not be harmed.' he declared. 'But if he is evil he will die.'

This story can be found in 1 Kings

I0892116

WORDSEARCH

Answer the following questions. Then use your answers to complete the wordsearch opposite.

1. Which famous king was the father of Solomon?
2. Who was Solomon's mother?
3. Which priest anointed Solomon king?
4. Which prophet was also there?
5. Which instruments were played when Solomon was made king?
6. Who tried to become king?
7. Where was Solomon made king?
8. On which animal did Solomon ride?

B	I	M	U	L	E	F	L	J
Z	A	D	O	K	J	L	A	O
O	S	T	E	P	M	U	R	T
N	D	A	H	I	G	T	H	C
P	A	J	A	S	I	E	K	O
O	V	T	G	A	H	S	H	E
K	I	Z	H	N	O	E	I	C
U	D	M	S	A	N	J	B	U
E	H	A	J	I	N	O	D	A

MATCH THE PICTURES

erde

lfow

tosga

peseh

srohse

teclat

Decode the words and match them to the right picture.

Join the numbers and colour in the picture

SOLOMON'S DREAM

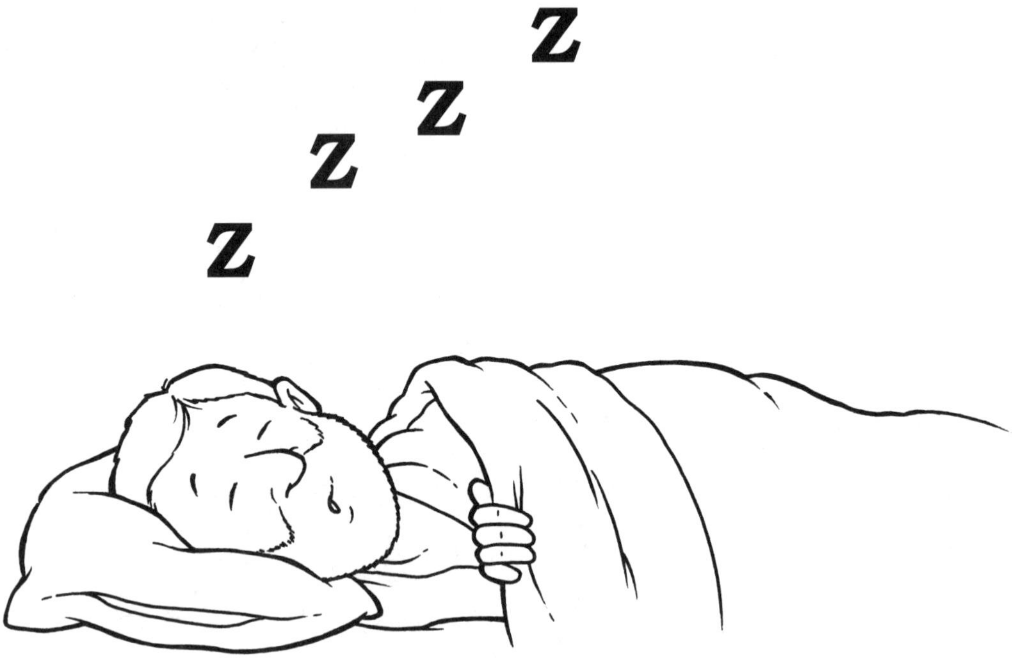

One night, when Solomon was asleep, God spoke to him in a dream. 'Ask for whatever you want me to give you,' he said.

You can read this story is in 1 Kings 3.

Unscramble the letters to see what Solomon could have asked for:

1. **g o n l f l i e** _ _ _ _ _ _ _ _

2. **h e s c i r** _ _ _ _ _ _

3. **t h e d a f o n e s i e me** _ _ _ _ _ _ _ _ _ _ _ _ _ _

Using the letters in the picture above, fill in the gaps and find out David's advice to Solomon before he died.

Be s _ _ _ _ g

Do what the Lord your God a _ _ s

Keep God's l _ w _

ANIMALS
in Solomon's kingdom

How many different kinds of animals can you see? Colour in the picture and find out more from the Bible in 1 Kings 4.

WORD PUZZLE

ACROSS

1. The wise king.
3. Opposite of young.
6. The king had lots of these.
7. Opposite of good.
9. Country where the king lived.
10. The king was this when God spoke to him.

DOWN

1. The king asked God for this.
2. Opposite of yes.
4. The king's father.
5. Used for building.
8. Very weak.

SOLOMON'S WISDOM

One day, two women came to Solomon. One of them said, 'My Lord, I live in a house with this woman. We both had baby sons, but during the night this woman's son died. When she saw that her son was dead, she put him in bed with me. Then she took my child and pretended that he was hers. In the morning when I woke up, I looked closely at the baby and knew that she had tricked me.'

The two women began to argue. Each one declared that the living baby belonged to her. What should King Solomon do?

Wise Solomon had a plan. 'Bring me a sword,' he said. 'Cut the living baby in two. Give half to one woman and half to the other.'

The woman whose son was alive said, 'Please my Lord. Give her the living baby. Don't kill him.' But the other said, 'Neither of us shall have him. Cut him in two!'

Then King Solomon knew that the first woman was the real mother. He ordered that the baby should be given to her.

All the people were amazed by Solomon's great wisdom.

You can read this story in 1 Kings 3.

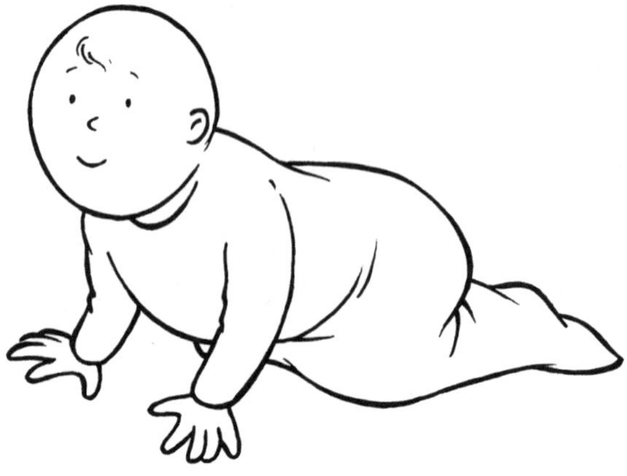

Can you spot the differences?
Once you've found them.
colour in the pictures.

WORD PUZZLE

My first is in Nathan and Sheba and three
My second in olive, but not in tree
My third is in ruby, in silver not gold
My fourth is in bath, in basin not bowl
My fifth is in trumpet, not flute or sing
The answer will give you the name of a king.

ANSWER: ____________________

Unscramble the letters to discover what Solomon used to build the temple and his palace. You'll find the answers in 1 Kings 6 and 7.

1. z r e b o n ____________________
2. d o g l ____________________
3. d e c a r d o w o ____________________
4. n o s e t ____________________
5. v i e l o o d o w ____________________
6. n e p i o o d w ____________________

MAZE

Find your way to the entrance of Solomon's temple

NUMBERS

Work out the following sums. When you have the answer, crack the code and reveal the name of Solomon's son who became king.

A	B	C	D	E	F	G	H	I
1	2	3	4	5	6	7	8	9

J	K	L	M	N	O	P	Q	R
10	11	12	13	14	15	16	17	18

S	T	U	V	W	X	Y	Z
19	20	21	22	23	24	25	26

1. Add together the number of years it took Solomon to build the temple and the royal palace (1 Kings 9:10). Subtract the number of cherubim in the inner sanctuary (1 Kings 6:23).
2. The number of stands on the south side of the temple (1 Kings 7:39).
3. The number of lions beside Solomon's throne (1 Kings 10:20) minus the number of years Solomon had reigned when he began building the temple (1 Kings 6:1).
4. The number of bulls in the temple plus the number of bulls facing the north (1 Kings 7:25).
5. The number of olive wood doors in the inner sanctuary of the temple (1 Kings 6:32).
6. The number of stall-fed cattle (1 Kings 4:23) plus the number of stands on the north side of the temple (1 Kings 7:39).
7. The number of steps leading to Solomon's throne (1 Kings 10:19) minus the number of gold lampstands on the left in front of the inner sanctuary (1 Kings 7:49).
8. The number of towns in Galilee which Solomon gave to Hiram (1 Kings 9:11) minus the number of years it took to build the temple (1 Kings 6:38b).

IMAGINE YOU ARE A REPORTER ...

You have been asked to write the front page story for the local paper, after hearing about the building of the temple. Think about the headline you would choose and the highlights from the story. Draw a picture of what the temple might look like.

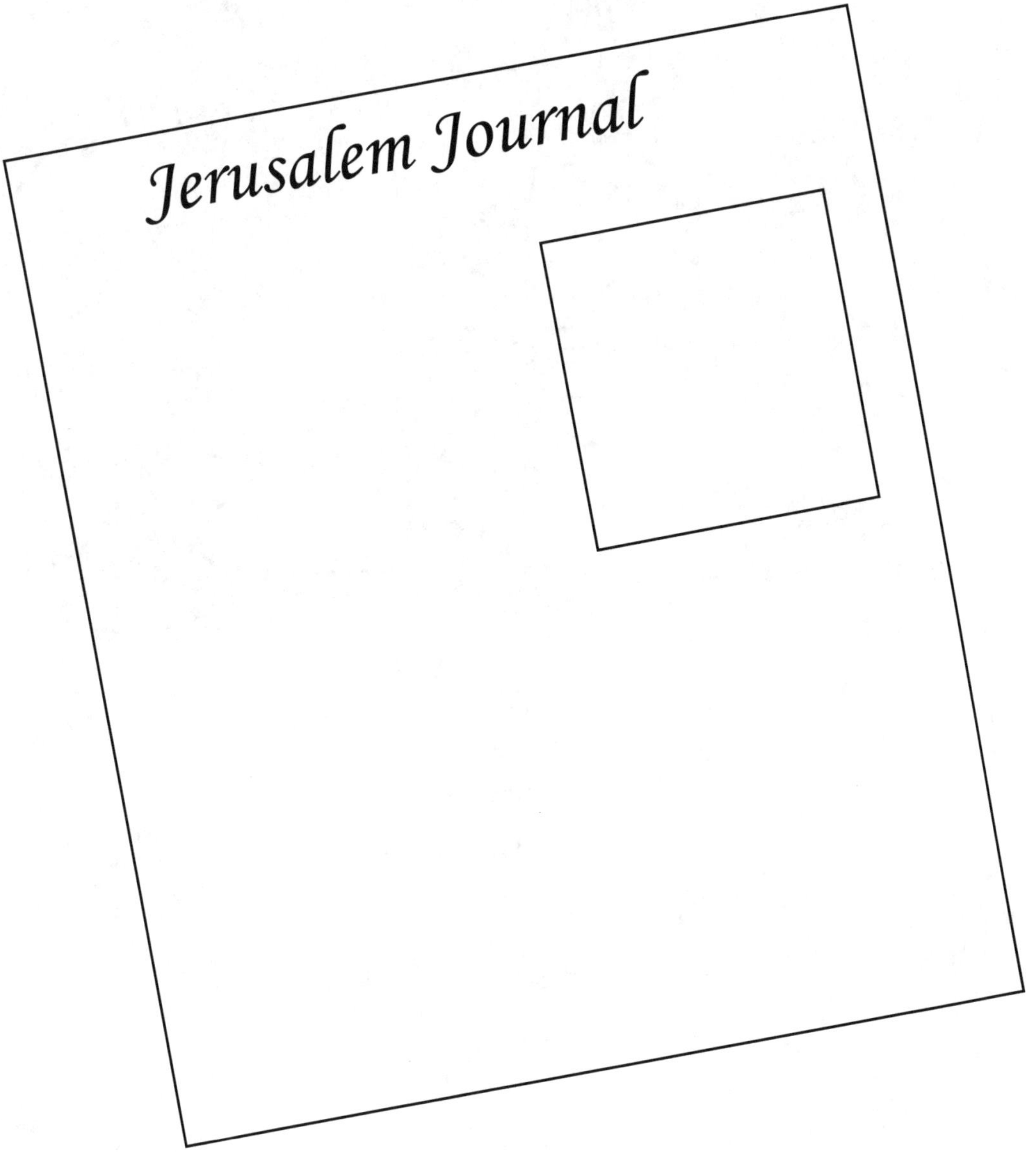

Join the numbers

THE VISIT OF THE QUEEN OF SHEBA

The Queen of Sheba heard of Solomon's great fame. She decided to visit Israel and ask him questions.

The queen arrived in Jerusalem with camels carrying spices, plenty of gold and precious stones. She asked Solomon many questions and nothing was too hard for him to explain to her.

She saw ...

his great wisdom,
the good food on his table,
his richly clothed servants
and the offerings he made to God.

It was truly amazing!

The queen said to Solomon, 'the things I heard in my country about your wisdom and all that you have done are true. But I did not believe it until I saw it with my own eyes. In fact it is better than I heard. How happy your men must be. Praise be to the Lord your God who has made you king.' And she gave the king large amounts of gold, spices and precious stones.

King Solomon gave the Queen of Sheba all that she asked for and more. Then she left and went back to her own country.

You can read this story in 1 Kings 10.

Work out the answers to the questions below and then fill them in on the grid opposite.

SOLVE THE PUZZLE

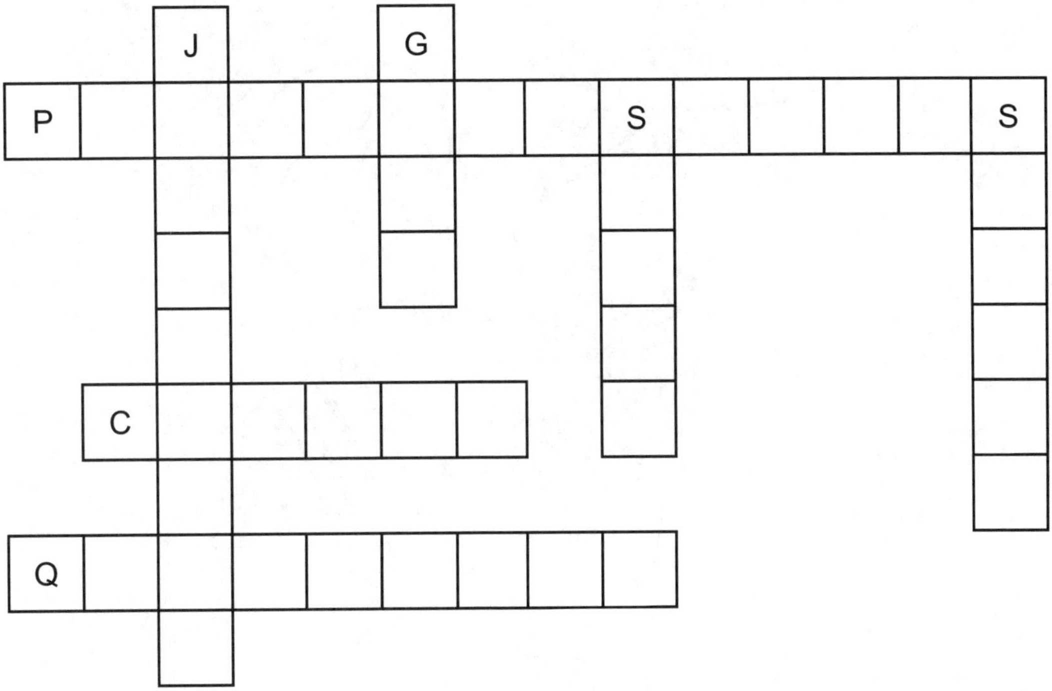

A	B	C	D	E	F	G	H	I	J	K	L	M
1	2	3	4	5	6	7	8	9	10	11	12	13
N	O	P	Q	R	S	T	U	V	W	X	Y	Z
14	15	16	17	18	19	20	21	22	23	24	25	26

1. Solomon reigned for 6, 15, 18, 20, 25 __________ years.

2. He had 19, 5, 22, 5, 14 ______________ 8, 21, 14, 4, 18, 5, 4 _______________ wives of royal birth.

3. Solomon's trading ships carried 7, 15, 12, 4 _________________ 19, 9, 12, 22, 5, 18 ___________ 9, 22, 15, 18, 25 ___________ 1, 16, 5, 19 _______ and 2, 1, 2, 15, 15, 14, 19 _____________.

4. Solomon had fourteen hundred 3, 8, 1, 18, 9, 15, 20, 19 ________ and twelve thousand 8, 15, 18, 19, 5, 19 ___________.

5. People who came to visit the king brought with them gifts of 19, 9, 12, 22, 5, 18 ___________ 7, 15, 12, 4 ___________ and 3, 12, 15, 20, 8, 5, 19 ________________.

6. The king's palace was called 20, 8, 5 _____ 16, 1, 12, 1, 3, 5 ___________ 15, 6 ___ 20, 8, 5 ____ 6, 15, 18, 5, 19, 20 __________ 15, 6 ___ 12, 5, 2, 1, 14, 15, 14 ________________.

7. Solomon wrote one 20, 8, 15, 21, 19, 1, 14, 4 _______________ and 6, 9, 22, 5 __________ songs.

8. He taught about 1, 14, 9, 13, 1, 12, 19 _________________ and 18, 5, 16, 20, 9, 12, 5, 19 ______________________________ and 6, 9, 19, 8 ____________.

9. He spoke three thousand 16, 18, 15, 22, 5, 18, 2, 19 __________.

10. King Solomon was greater in 18, 9, 3, 8, 5, 19 ____________ and 23, 9, 19, 4, 15, 13 _______________ than all the other kings of the earth.

SOLOMON AND PLACES

Use the code key to find out the place names. Then follow the footprints on the next page and fill in the gaps.

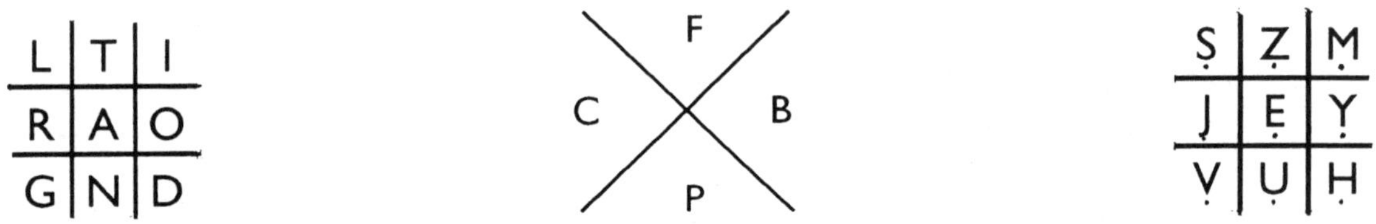

1.  and 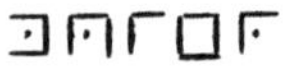
2. 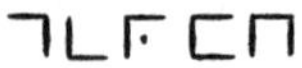
3. 
4. 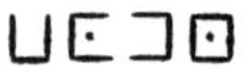
5. 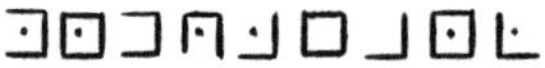
6. 
7. 
8. 
9. 
10. 

Made king over (1) _ _ _ _ _ _ and _ _ _ _ _
God appears to Solomon in a dream at _ _ _ _ _ _ (3)
Hiram king of (4)
_ _ _ _
Anointed at (2) _ _ _ _ _
Temple build in _ _ _ _ _ _ _ _ _ (5)
Palace of the Forest of _ _ _ _ _ _ _ built (6)
His ships bring back gold from (9) _ _ _ _ _
Solomon builds ships at (7) _ _ _ _ _ _ _ _ _ _
On the (8) _ _ _ _ _ _
Visit by the Queen of (10) _ _ _ _ _

Answers

Page 3: (1) (King) David, (2) Bathsheba, (3) Zadok, (4) Nathan, (5) trumpets and flutes, (6) Adonijah, (7) Gihon, (8) mule.

Page 4: (1) goats, (2) sheep, (3) horses, (4) deer, (5) cattle, (6) fowl.

Page 7: Solomon's dream: (1) long life, (2) riches, (3) death of enemies.
Fill in the gap: Be strong, do what the Lord your God asks,keep God's laws.

Page 8: Six.

Page 9. Across: (1) Solomom, (3) old, (6) cattle, (7) evil, (9) Israel (10) asleep.
Down: (1) spices, (2) no, (4) David, (5) stones, (8) frail.

Page 11: Pattern on vase, women's round necked tunic, king's necklace, women's necklace, women's apron, throne, extra bush, king holding something.

Page 12: Hiram
(1) bronze, (2) gold, (3) cedar wood, (4) stone, (5) olive wood, (6) pine wood.

Page 14: (1) 18 (2) 5 (3) 8 (4) 15 (5) 2 (6) 15 (7) 1 (8) 13
Rehoboam

Page 19: (1) Sheba, (2) Jerusalem, (3) spices, gold and precious stones, (4) camels, (5) questions.

Page 21: (1) forty, (2) seven hundred, (3) gold, silver, ivory, apes and baboons, (4) chariots and horses, (5) silver, gold and clothes, (6) The Palace of Lebanon, (7) one thousand and five, (8) animals and birds, reptiles and fish, (9) proverbs, (10) riches and wisdom.

Page 23: (1) Israel and Judah, (2) Gihon, (3) Gibeon, (4) Tyre, (5) Jerusalem, (6) Lebanon, (7) Ezion Geber, (8) Red Sea, (9) Ophir, (10) Sheba.

Text by Ros Woodman
Illustrations by David Wilson
ISBN 978-1-84550-404-5
© 1995 Christian Focus Publications
Reprinted 2008
Published by Christian Focus Publications, Geanies House, Fearn, Ross-shire, IV20 1TW, Scotland, U.K.
Printed and bound by Bell and Bain, Glasgow

The text and answers are based on the New International Version of the Bible